Snowmen

1 package (20 ounces) refrigerated chocolate chip cookie dough
1½ cups sifted powdered sugar
2 tablespoons milk
Candy corn, gumdrops, chocolate chips, licorice and other assorted small candies

1. Preheat oven to 375°F. Remove dough from wrapper. Cut dough into 12 equal sections. Divide each section into 3 balls: large, medium and small.

2. For each snowman, place 3 balls (small, medium and large) in row, ¼ inch apart, on ungreased cookie sheet.

3. Bake 10 to 12 minutes or until edges are very lightly browned. Cool 4 minutes on cookie sheets. Remove to wire racks to cool completely.

4. Mix powdered sugar and milk in medium bowl until smooth. Pour over cookies. Let cookies stand 20 minutes or until set.

5. Decorate with assorted candies to create snowman faces, hats and arms.   *Makes 1 dozen cookies*

Peanut Butter Chocolate Chippers

1 cup packed light brown sugar
1 cup creamy or chunky peanut butter
1 egg
¾ cup milk chocolate chips
   Granulated sugar

1. Preheat oven to 350°F.

2. Beat brown sugar, peanut butter and egg in medium bowl with electric mixer at medium speed until well blended. Add chocolate chips; stir well.

3. Shape heaping tablespoonfuls of dough into 1½-inch balls. Place balls 2 inches apart on ungreased cookie sheets.

4. Dip fork into granulated sugar; press criss-cross fashion onto each ball, flattening to ½-inch thickness.

5. Bake 12 minutes or until set. Cool on cookie sheets 2 minutes. Remove to wire racks to cool completely.

Makes about 2 dozen cookies

Note: This simple recipe is unusual because it doesn't contain any flour—but it still makes great cookies!

Date Pinwheel Cookies

1¼ cups dates, pitted and finely chopped
¾ cup orange juice
½ cup granulated sugar
1 tablespoon butter
3 cups plus 1 tablespoon all-purpose flour, divided
2 teaspoons vanilla, divided
1 cup packed brown sugar
4 ounces cream cheese
¼ cup shortening
2 eggs
1 teaspoon baking soda
½ teaspoon salt

1. Mix dates, juice, granulated sugar, butter and 1 tablespoon flour in saucepan over medium heat. Cook and stir 10 minutes or until thick; remove from heat. Stir in 1 teaspoon vanilla; set aside to cool.

2. Beat brown sugar, cream cheese and shortening in large bowl with electric mixer at medium speed about 3 minutes or until fluffy. Add eggs and remaining 1 teaspoon vanilla; beat 2 minutes.

3. Mix remaining 3 cups flour, baking soda and salt in bowl. Add to shortening mixture; stir just until blended. Divide dough in half. Roll half of dough on lightly floured surface into 12×9-inch rectangle. Spread half of date mixture evenly over dough, leaving ¼-inch border at top short edge. Starting at short side, tightly roll up dough jelly-roll style. Wrap in plastic wrap; freeze at least 1 hour. Repeat with remaining dough and date mixture.

4. Preheat oven to 350°F. Grease cookie sheets. Unwrap dough. Using heavy thread or dental floss, cut dough into ¼-inch slices. Place slices 1 inch apart on prepared cookie sheets.

5. Bake 12 minutes or until golden. Cool on cookie sheets 2 minutes. Remove to wire racks; cool completely.   *Makes 6 dozen cookies*

Yuletide Linzer Bars

1⅓ cups butter, softened
¾ cup granulated sugar
1 egg
1 teaspoon grated lemon peel
2½ cups all-purpose flour
1½ cups whole almonds, ground
1 teaspoon ground cinnamon
¾ cup raspberry preserves
Powdered sugar

1. Preheat oven to 350°F. Grease 13×9-inch baking pan.

2. Beat butter and granulated sugar in large bowl with electric mixer at medium speed until light and fluffy. Beat in egg and lemon peel until well blended. Stir in flour, ground almonds and cinnamon until well blended.

3. Press 2 cups dough onto bottom of prepared pan. Spread preserves over crust. Press remaining dough, small amount at a time, evenly over preserves.

4. Bake 35 to 40 minutes or until golden brown. Cool completely in pan on wire rack. Sprinkle with powdered sugar; cut into bars.

Makes 36 bars

Fruitcake Slices

1 cup (2 sticks) butter, softened
1 cup powdered sugar
1 egg
1 teaspoon vanilla
1½ cups coarsely chopped candied fruit (fruitcake mix)
½ cup coarsely chopped walnuts
2½ cups all-purpose flour, divided
¾ to 1 cup flaked coconut
   Maraschino cherry halves (optional)

1. Beat butter and powdered sugar in large bowl with electric mixer at medium speed until light and fluffy. Add egg and vanilla; beat until well blended.

2. Combine candied fruit and walnuts in medium bowl. Stir ¼ cup flour into fruit mixture. Add remaining 2¼ cups flour to butter mixture; beat until well blended. Stir in fruit mixture with spoon.

3. Shape dough into 2 logs, each about 2 inches in diameter and 5½ inches long. Spread coconut evenly on sheet of waxed paper. Roll logs in coconut, coating evenly. Wrap each log in plastic wrap. Refrigerate 2 to 3 hours or overnight, or freeze up to 1 month. (Let frozen logs stand at room temperature about 10 minutes before slicing and baking.)

4. Preheat oven to 350°F. Grease cookie sheets. Cut logs into ¼-inch-thick slices; place 1 inch apart on prepared cookie sheets.

5. Bake 13 to 15 minutes or until edges are golden brown. Remove to wire racks to cool. Decorate with cherry halves, if desired. Store in airtight container.

Makes about 4 dozen cookies

Festive Candy Canes

¾ cup (1½ sticks) butter, softened
1 cup powdered sugar
1 egg
1 teaspoon peppermint extract
½ teaspoon vanilla
1⅔ cups all-purpose flour
⅛ teaspoon salt
    Red food coloring

1. Preheat oven to 350°F. Beat butter and powdered sugar in large bowl with electric mixer at medium speed until light and fluffy. Add egg, peppermint extract and vanilla; beat until well blended. Add flour and salt; beat until well blended. (Dough will be sticky.)

2. Divide dough in half. Tint half of dough with food coloring to desired shade of red. Leave remaining dough plain.

3. For each candy cane, with floured hands, shape heaping teaspoonful dough of each color into 5-inch rope; twist together into candy cane shape. Place 2 inches apart on ungreased cookie sheet.

4. Bake 7 to 8 minutes or just until set and edges are very lightly browned. Let cookies stand on cookie sheets 2 minutes. Remove to wire racks to cool completely.   *Makes about 2 dozen cookies*

Decadent Brownies

½ cup dark corn syrup
½ cup (1 stick) butter
 6 squares (1 ounce each) semisweet chocolate
¾ cup sugar
 3 eggs
 1 cup all-purpose flour
 1 cup chopped walnuts
 1 teaspoon vanilla
    Fudge Glaze (recipe follows)

1. Preheat oven to 350°F. Grease 8-inch square baking pan.

2. Combine corn syrup, butter and chocolate in large heavy saucepan over low heat. Stir until chocolate is melted and mixture is well blended. Remove from heat; blend in sugar. Stir in eggs, flour, walnuts and vanilla. Spread batter evenly in prepared pan.

3. Bake 20 to 25 minutes or just until center is set. *Do not overbake.* Meanwhile, prepare Fudge Glaze. Remove brownies from oven. Immediately spread glaze evenly over hot brownies. Cool in pan on wire rack. Cut into 2-inch squares.   *Makes 16 brownies*

Fudge Glaze

 3 squares (1 ounce each) semisweet chocolate
 2 tablespoons dark corn syrup
 1 tablespoon butter
 1 teaspoon light cream or milk

Combine chocolate, corn syrup and butter in small heavy saucepan. Stir over low heat until chocolate is melted; stir in cream until smooth and well blended.

Almond Milk Chocolate Chippers

½ cup slivered almonds
1¼ cups all-purpose flour
½ teaspoon baking soda
½ teaspoon salt
½ cup (1 stick) butter, softened
½ cup packed light brown sugar
⅓ cup granulated sugar
1 egg
2 tablespoons almond-flavored liqueur
1 cup milk chocolate chips

1. Preheat oven to 350°F. To toast almonds, spread on ungreased cookie sheet. Bake 8 to 10 minutes or until golden brown, stirring frequently. Remove almonds from cookie sheet; set aside to cool.

2. *Increase oven temperature to 375°F.* Combine flour, baking soda and salt in small bowl.

3. Beat butter, brown sugar and granulated sugar in large bowl with electric mixer at medium speed until creamy. Add egg and liqueur; beat until well blended. Gradually add flour mixture, beating until well blended. Stir in chocolate chips and almonds.

4. Drop dough by rounded teaspoonfuls 2 inches apart onto ungreased cookie sheets.

5. Bake 9 to 10 minutes or until edges are golden brown. Let stand on cookie sheets 2 minutes. Remove cookies to wire racks to cool completely. Store tightly covered at room temperature or freeze up to 3 months. *Makes about 3 dozen cookies*

Jolly Peanut Butter Gingerbread Cookies

1⅔ cups (10-ounce package) REESE'S® Peanut Butter Chips
¾ cup (1½ sticks) butter or margarine, softened
1 cup packed light brown sugar
1 cup dark corn syrup
2 eggs
5 cups all-purpose flour
1 teaspoon baking soda
½ teaspoon ground cinnamon
¼ teaspoon ground ginger
¼ teaspoon salt

1. Place peanut butter chips in small microwave-safe bowl. Microwave at HIGH (100%) 1 to 2 minutes or until chips are melted when stirred. Beat melted peanut butter chips and butter in large bowl until well blended. Add brown sugar, corn syrup and eggs; beat until fluffy.

2. Stir together flour, baking soda, cinnamon, ginger and salt. Add half of flour mixture to butter mixture; beat on low speed of mixer until smooth. With wooden spoon, stir in remaining flour mixture until well blended. Divide into thirds; wrap each in plastic wrap. Refrigerate at least 1 hour or until dough is firm enough to roll.

3. Heat oven to 325°F.

4. Roll 1 dough portion at a time to ⅛-inch thickness on lightly floured surface; with floured cookie cutters, cut into holiday shapes. Place on ungreased cookie sheet.

5. Bake 10 to 12 minutes or until set and lightly browned. Cool slightly; remove from cookie sheet to wire rack. Cool completely. Frost and decorate as desired.   *Makes about 6 dozen cookies*

Jolly Peanut Butter Gingerbread Cookies

Slice 'n' Bake Ginger Wafers

1 cup packed brown sugar
½ cup (1 stick) butter, softened
¼ cup light molasses
1 egg
2 teaspoons ground ginger
1 teaspoon grated orange peel
¼ teaspoon salt
¼ teaspoon ground cinnamon
¼ teaspoon ground cloves
2 cups all-purpose flour

1. Beat brown sugar, butter and molasses in large bowl with electric mixer at medium speed until creamy. Add egg, ginger, orange peel, salt, cinnamon and cloves; beat until well blended. Stir in flour until well blended. (Dough will be very stiff.)

2. Shape dough into 2 logs, each about 1½ inches in diameter and 8 inches long. Wrap each log in plastic wrap; refrigerate at least 5 hours or up to 3 days.

3. Preheat oven to 350°F. Cut dough into ¼-inch-thick slices. Place about 2 inches apart on ungreased baking sheets. Bake 12 to 14 minutes or until set. Remove to wire racks; cool completely.

Makes about 4½ dozen cookies

Tip: Dip half of each cookie in melted white chocolate, or drizzle cookies with a glaze of 1¼ cups powdered sugar and 2 tablespoons orange juice. Or, cut cookie dough into ⅛-inch-thick slices and bake. Sandwich melted caramel candy or peanut butter between cooled cookies.

Slice 'n' Bake Ginger Wafers

Danish Cookie Rings

½ cup blanched almonds
2 cups all-purpose flour
¾ cup sugar
¼ teaspoon baking powder
1 cup (2 sticks) butter, cut into small pieces
1 egg
1 tablespoon milk
1 tablespoon vanilla
15 candied red cherries
15 candied green cherries

1. Grease cookie sheets; set aside. Process almonds in food processor until ground, but not pasty. Combine almonds, flour, sugar and baking powder in large bowl. Cut butter into flour mixture with pastry blender or 2 knives until mixture is crumbly.

2. Beat egg, milk and vanilla in small bowl with fork until well blended. Add egg mixture to flour mixture; stir until soft dough forms.

3. Spoon dough into pastry bag fitted with medium star tip. Pipe 3-inch rings 2 inches apart on prepared cookie sheets. Refrigerate rings 15 minutes or until firm.

4. Preheat oven to 375°F. Cut red cherries into quarters. Cut green cherries into halves; cut each half into 4 slivers. Press red cherry quarter onto each ring where ends meet. Arrange 2 green cherry slivers on either side of red cherry to form leaves. Bake 8 to 10 minutes or until golden. Remove cookies to wire racks to cool completely. Store tightly covered at room temperature or freeze up to 3 months. *Makes about 5 dozen cookies*

Pumpkin White Chocolate Drops

2 cups (4 sticks) butter, softened
2 cups granulated sugar
1 can (16 ounces) solid-pack pumpkin
2 eggs
4 cups all-purpose flour
2 teaspoons pumpkin pie spice*
1 teaspoon baking powder
½ teaspoon baking soda
1 package (12 ounces) white chocolate chips
1 container (16 ounces) cream cheese frosting
¼ cup packed brown sugar

*Substitute 1 teaspoon ground cinnamon, ½ teaspoon ground ginger and ¼ teaspoon each ground allspice and ground nutmeg for 2 teaspoons pumpkin pie spice.

1. Preheat oven to 375°F. Grease cookie sheets.

2. Beat butter and granulated sugar in large bowl with electric mixer at medium speed until light and fluffy. Add pumpkin and eggs; beat until well blended. Add flour, pumpkin pie spice, baking powder and baking soda; beat just until blended. Stir in white chocolate chips.

3. Drop dough by teaspoonfuls about 2 inches apart onto prepared cookie sheets. Bake about 16 minutes or until set and bottoms are browned. Cool 1 minute on cookie sheets. Remove to wire racks to cool completely.

4. Combine frosting and brown sugar in small bowl. Spread on warm cookies.   *Makes about 6 dozen cookies*

Pumpkin White Chocolate Drops

Mocha Crinkles

1⅓ cups packed light brown sugar
½ cup vegetable oil
¼ cup sour cream
1 egg
1 teaspoon vanilla
1¾ cups all-purpose flour
¾ cup unsweetened cocoa powder
2 teaspoons instant espresso or coffee granules
1 teaspoon baking soda
¼ teaspoon salt
⅛ teaspoon black pepper
½ cup powdered sugar

1. Beat brown sugar and oil in large bowl with electric mixer at medium speed until well blended. Add sour cream, egg and vanilla; beat until well blended.

2. Combine flour, cocoa, espresso, baking soda, salt and pepper in medium bowl. Add flour mixture to brown sugar mixture; beat until well blended. Cover dough; refrigerate 3 to 4 hours or until firm.

3. Preheat oven to 350°F. Place powdered sugar in shallow bowl. Shape dough into 1-inch balls. Roll balls in powdered sugar; place 2 inches apart on ungreased cookie sheets.

4. Bake 10 to 12 minutes or until tops of cookies are firm. *Do not overbake.* Remove to wire racks to cool completely.

Makes about 6 dozen cookies

Christmas Tree Platter

1 recipe Christmas Cookie Dough (page 30)
2 cups sifted powdered sugar
2 tablespoons milk or lemon juice
   Assorted food colorings, colored sugars and assorted
      small decors

1. Prepare Christmas Cookie Dough.

2. Preheat oven to 350°F. Roll half of dough to ⅛-inch thickness on lightly floured surface. Cut dough with lightly floured tree-shaped cookie cutters. Place on ungreased cookie sheets.

3. Bake 10 to 12 minutes or until edges are lightly browned. Remove to wire racks to cool completely.

4. Repeat with remaining half of dough. Reroll scraps; cut into small circles for ornaments, squares and rectangles for gift boxes and tree trunks.

5. Bake 8 to 12 minutes, depending on size of cookies, until edges are lightly browned.

6. For icing, combine sugar and milk in medium bowl. Tint most of icing green and a smaller amount red or other colors for ornaments and boxes. Spread green icing on trees. Sprinkle ornaments and boxes with colored sugars or decorate as desired. Arrange cookies on flat platter to resemble tree as shown in photo.

Makes about 1 dozen cookies

Tip: Use this beautiful Christmas Tree Platter cookie as your centerpiece for this holiday's family dinner. It's sure to receive lots of "oohs" and "ahs!"

continued on page 30

Christmas Tree Platter

Christmas Tree Platter, continued

Christmas Cookie Dough

2¼ cups all-purpose flour
¼ teaspoon salt
1 cup sugar
¾ cup (1½ sticks) butter, softened
1 egg
1 teaspoon vanilla
1 teaspoon almond extract

1. Combine flour and salt in medium bowl.

2. Beat sugar and butter in large bowl with electric mixer at medium speed until light and fluffy. Add egg, vanilla and almond extract; beat until well blended. Gradually add flour mixture to butter mixture. Beat until well blended.

3. Shape dough into 2 discs; wrap in plastic wrap and refrigerate 30 minutes or until firm.